WHAT IS GOD SAYING TO YOU?

A Journey Through
The Book of Proverbs

RABBI GREG HERSHBERG

OlivePress
צהר זית
Publisher

WHAT IS GOD SAYING TO YOU?

A Journey Through
The Book of Proverbs

RABBI GREG HERSHBERG

WHAT IS GOD SAYING TO YOU?

A Journey Through The Book of Proverbs

Copyright © 2022 by Rabbi Greg Hershberg

Printed in the USA

ISBN 978-1-941173-54-1

Front and back cover photos, ID 136738631 © Helen Hotson | Shutterstock.com.
Author's portrait, copyright © 2021 by Larry Falls, Macon, Georgia.
Cover design, copyright © 2022 by Roxsanne Roush.

Published by

Olive Press Messianic and Christian Publisher
www.olivepresspublisher.com
www.olivepresspublishers.com
olivepressbooks@gmail.com

Messianic & Christian Publisher

Our prayer at Olive Press is that we may help make the Word of Adonai fully known, that it spread rapidly and be glorified everywhere. We hope our books help open people's eyes so they will turn from darkness to Light and from the power of the adversary to God and to trust in יֵשׁוּעַ Yeshua (Jesus). (From II Thess. 3:1; Col. 1:25; Acts 26:18,15 NRSV *New Revised Standard Version* and CJB) May the Lord use this book in particular to reveal Himself in a mighty way to each reader.

PROVERBS – WHAT IS GOD SAYING TO YOU?

CONTENTS

CHAPTER 1

INTRODUCTION

It was June 19, 2021. I was off to my old stomping ground, Long Beach New York, for somewhat of a sabbatical. It would be the first time in my adult working life that I would be taking an extended leave from my customary work. I had no idea what to expect, but I was very excited. I was hopeful that this was what God wanted and what I needed. All systems were a go, as God had set things up like only He could have, to make the dream a reality.

I arrived in Long Beach at midnight, and although I was excited to see the beach, I was all the more excited to get up first thing in the morning and commune with God by reading The Bible. I woke up early Sunday morning, grabbed my Bible and all of a sudden I thought to myself, what should I read? Should I read a particular section? Should I study something topically? Maybe I'll just wing it and open up the Bible at random? I was faced with a dilemma.

You must understand that Sunday morning is sacred to me. I get up early every Sunday morning and the Lord gives me direction regarding a subject matter that He would like me to teach on for the upcoming Shabbat. Then the Holy Spirit navigates me through the Bible in order to direct me to the scriptures that support the subject. It ends up being a beautiful Spirit led study. But here I was needing nothing to teach on for the next six weeks, and I found myself at a loss. I felt like a fish out of water. It was incredibly uncomfortable and if I may say, downright strange. So of course, I prayed and sought the Lord for direction. He told me that this is the way most believers feel when it comes to reading the Bible. He said that they really do have the desire to read, but they just don't know what to read. I was shocked, because for years I have exhorted, encouraged, even pushed people to read their Bibles. I had no idea that although people want to read their Bible, they have no idea, direction, or plan, on what to read.

So I thought, here I am, not Rabbi Greg seeking the Lord for a subject to teach others, but just Greg seeking the Lord for a subject to teach myself. He emphatically said *"Proverbs."* He said I was to read the Proverbs chapter that corresponded to the numerical day of the month. Because it was June 20th, I would read the 20th chapter of Proverbs. Interestingly enough because there are 31 chapters in the book of Proverbs, it would work out perfectly. He then said that I would need paper and pen because as I read the chapter, He would make a verse or verses jump off the page for me. I was to write the verse, or verses down, along with a devotional meditation of sorts that would just come to me, via the Holy Spirit. You can imagine just how excited I was. Yes! I have direction. I have a plan. Hallelujah!

Just when I was ready to roll, He dropped a bomb on me. He said I was to write it in book form and share it with others. I said, "Oh no, Lord, not work." I so desperately wanted to just decompress and disconnect from being Rabbi Greg. He said you will have plenty of time to kick back and relax, but for the next 31 mornings you will write it down. Think of how many others will benefit from having a reading plan.

Now if you already have a daily reading plan, by all means feel free to continue with it. But If you don't, please put this plan to the test. I did, and it was remarkable to say the least. When you're reading the book of Proverbs, not only are you reading the greatest book ever written on how to live a successful life, but you are reading the greatest book ever written on the subject of wisdom. The Holy Spirit promises to tailor it and personalize it to your very own life. Wow! The Word of God, infused by the Spirit of God, brings the Presence of God.

Now before we embark on our journey together, we need to talk about the amazing, wonderful, magnificent book we call "Proverbs."

Chapter 2

THE PURPOSE OF PROVERBS

The book of Proverbs is timeless. It is as applicable today as it was 3,000 years ago. It deals with the problems of life that each of us has to face.

Proverbs is the world's finest collection of sound, sanctified common sense, written so that young people might not have to make some of the sad, sorrowful mistakes their elders have made. The purpose of Proverbs is stated up front in the very first chapter, verses one through seven, "The proverbs of Shlomo the son of David, king of Isra'el, are for learning about wisdom and discipline; for understanding words expressing deep insight; for gaining an intelligently disciplined life, doing what is right, just and fair; for endowing with caution those who don't think and the young person with knowledge and discretion. Someone who is already wise will hear and learn still more; someone who already understands will gain the ability to counsel well; he will understand proverbs, obscure expressions, the sayings and riddles of the wise. The fear of ADONAI is the beginning of knowledge, but fools despise wisdom and discipline." (Prov. 1:1-7).

It is to give wisdom and understanding to a young man so that he will find true blessedness in life and escape the snares and pitfalls of sin. The key verse of the book is verse seven of chapter one. "The fear of ADONAI is the beginning of knowledge." If a man wants to be wise, the place to begin is in reverencing God, which is trusting and obeying Him. What is more reasonable than that the creature should trust his Creator? On the other hand, what is more illogical than for a man to reject God's Word and to live by his own hunches?

The second part of the verse says, "But fools despise wisdom and discipline." Just as a wise man in this book is one who is willing and anxious to learn, a fool is one who cannot be told anything. He is unmanageable and conceited, and only learns lessons the hard way, if at all.

A proverb is a brief but forceful and meaningful statement of wisdom, often worded in a skillful way to make it easy to remember. Most of the proverbs consist of two clauses, presenting either similarities or contrasts.

There are several varieties of proverbs, as follows:

1. Some are single statements, expressing a simple fact: "When a man's ways please ADONAI, He makes even the man's enemies be at peace with him." (Proverbs 16:7).

2. Some consist of two clauses or phrases in which one thing is compared to another: "Like cold water to a person faint from thirst is good news from a distant land." (Proverbs 25:25).

3. Still others have two clauses or phrases, usually connected by *but,* and describing things that are opposite to each other. "The memory of the righteous will be for a blessing, but the reputation of the wicked will rot." (Proverbs 10:7)

4. There are proverbs with two clauses or phrases in which the same thought is repeated in a slightly different way: "A prostitute is a deep ditch, and a forbidden woman like a narrow well." (Proverbs 23:27)

King Solomon is the principal author of the Book of Proverbs. His name appears in Proverbs 1:1, 10:1, and 25:1. The Hebrew title *maw-shawl Shelomo* is translated into English as "*The Proverbs of Solomon.*" The Proverbs were penned around 900 BC during Solomon's reign as King. During Solomon's reign, the nation of Israel reached its pinnacle spiritually, politically, culturally, and economically. Solomon's reputation was so great that many foreign dignitaries from all over the world came to listen to his wisdom, "People from all nations came to hear the wisdom of Shlomo, including kings from all over the earth who had never heard of his wisdom." (I Kings 4:34).

The Book of Proverbs teaches us the mind of God in matters high and lofty, as well as in matters common and ordinary. It covers a wide range of subjects – from spanking a child to ruling a kingdom. It covers subjects like personal conduct, sexual relations, business, wealth, charity, ambition, discipline, debt, child-rearing, character, alcohol, politics, revenge, and godliness. One has to wonder if there is any truth that is not found here.

It covers issues like installment buying, juvenile delinquency, and labor management. You will meet all kinds of people here—the brawling woman, the proud fool, the man who does not like to be told his faults, and the ideal wife. And best of all, the Messiah is here, speaking to us as wisdom personified. Wisdom is mentioned 200 times in the Bible, 50 times alone in the Book of Proverbs. We are continually being exhorted throughout the Bible to seek wisdom. The beauty of Proverbs is in it's undeniable practicality. Proverbs is the greatest "How To" book ever written.

There are two recurring themes in the Bible, namely wisdom and knowledge. They are related but not synonymous. Wisdom is the ability to discern what is true, right, and lasting. Knowledge, on the other hand, is information gained through experience, study, and investigation. Knowledge can exist without wisdom, but wisdom cannot exist without knowledge. God wants us to know Him and what He expects of us. Knowledge of God's commandments is good, but applying those commandments in our lives is what

God is truly after. The book of Proverbs is the best place in the Bible to learn biblical wisdom. Once you understand something, you gain knowledge. Once you put that knowledge into practice, you attain wisdom. Knowledge memorizes the Ten Commandments; wisdom obeys them. Knowledge learns of God, wisdom loves Him.

Proverbs is difficult to outline. Instead of presenting a continuity of thought, like a motion picture, it presents individual pictures. With that being said, I would like to classify some of the subjects in the book of Proverbs.

CHAPTER 3

CLASSIFICATION OF SOME OF THE SUBJECTS IN THE BOOK OF PROVERBS

The Lord
The blessing of (10:22)
Confidence in (3:25, 26)
Creation by (3:19, 20; 16:4; 20:12; 22:2b;
    29:13b)
Discipline of (3:11, 12)
The fear of (1:7, 29; 2:5; 8:13; 9:10; 10:27;
    14:26, 27; 15:16, 33; 16:6; 19:23; 22:4;
    23:17; 24:21; 28:14)
Guidance of (3:5, 6; 16:3, 9)
Judgment and justice by (15:25a; 17:3; 21:2;
    29:26)

Omnipresence of (15:3)
Omniscience of (15:11; 16:2)
Prayer answered by (15:8, 29)
Protection by (15:25b; 18:10)
Source of wisdom (2:6-8)
Sovereignty and power of (16:1, 7, 9, 33;
     19:21; 20:24; 21:30, 31; 22:12)
To be trusted (29:25b)

Parenting
Instruction in child training (13:24; 19:18;
     22:6, 15; 23:13, 14; 29:15, 17)
Obedience and disobedience to parents
     (1:8, 9; 6:20, 22; 13:1, 19-26; 20:20; 23:22;
     30:17)
Words of parental advice (1:8-19; 2:1-22; 3:1-
     35; 4:1-27; 5:1-23; 6:1-35; 7:1-27; 23:19-
     35; 24:4-22; 31:1-9)

Speech
Appropriate (15:23; 25:11)
Backbiting (25:23)
Belittling (11:12a)
Disturbing (27:14)
Evil (12:13a; 15:28b)
Excessive (10:19a; 13:3b)
Flattering (20:19; 26:28b; 28:23; 29:5)
Foolish (12:23b; 14:3a, 7; 15:2b; 18:6, 7)
Gentle (15:1a, 4a)

Good (10:20a, 21a; 16:21, 23, 24; 23:16)
Harmful (11:9, 11; 12:18a; 15:4b; 16:27;
    18:21; 26:18, 19)
Harsh (15:1b)
Hasty (18:13; 29:20)
Healing (12:18b; 15:4a; 16:24; 18:21)
Honest (12:19a; 13:5)
Inappropriate (17:7)
Lying, deceitful (6:17; 10:18a; 12:19b, 22a,
    14:25b; 17:4; 26:18, 19, 23-26, 28a)
Perverse (4:24; 10:31b, 32b; 15:4b; 17:20b)
Restrained (10:19b; 11:12b, 13b; 12:23a;
    13:3a; 17:27a, 28; 21:23)
Satisfying (12:14; 18:20)
Slanderous (10:18b; 30:10)
Tale bearing, gossiping (11:13a; 16:28; 17:9b;
    18:8; 20:19; 22:11a; 26:10, 22-26, 28)
Thoughtful (15:28a)
True and false witness (6:19; 12:17; 14:5, 25;
    19:5, 9, 28; 21:28; 25:18)
Wise (10:31a; 14:3b; 15:2a; 18:4)
Worthless (14:23b)

Various Themes
Abominations
– to the Lord (3:32; 6:16; 8:7; 11:1, 20; 12:22;
    15:8, 9, 26; 16:5; 17:15; 20:10, 23; 21:27;
    28:9)
– to others (13:19; 16:12; 24:9; 26:25; 29:27)

Ancient landmarks (22:28; 23:10, 11)
Borrowing and lending (22:7b)
The diligent man (21:5; 22:29; 27:18, 23-27;
    28:19a)
The diligent man and the sluggard contrasted
    (10:4, 5; 12:24, 27; 13:4)
Enemy (16:7; 24:17, 18; 25:21; 27:6)
Envy (3:31; 14:30; 23:17; 24:1, 19; 27:4)
False balanced and weights (11:1; 16:11;
    20:10, 23)
Friends, neighbors, and friendship (3:27-29;
    6:1-5; 11:12; 12:26; 14:21; 16:28; 17:9, 17;
    18:17, 24; 21:10; 22:24, 25; 24:17, 19;
    25:8, 9, 17, 20, 21, 22; 26:18, 19; 27:6, 9,
    10, 14, 17; 28:23; 29:5)
Honey (16:24; 24:13; 25:16, 27; 27:7)
Industriousness (12:9, 11; 14:4, 23a)
The interrelationship between physical,
    mental, and spiritual health (3:1, 2, 7, 8, 16;
    4:10, 22; 9:11; 13:12; 14:30; 15:13; 30,
    16:24; 17:22; 18:14; 27:9)
Justice and injustice (13:23; 17:15, 26; 18:5;
    21:15; 22:8, 16; 24:23, 24)
The king or ruler (14:28, 35; 16:10, 12-15;
    19:12; 20:2, 8, 26, 28; 21:1; 22:11, 29;
    23:1; 24:21, 22; 25:2-7, 15; 28:15, 16; 29:2,
    4, 12, 14, 26; 30:31; 31:4, 5)
The lot (16:33; 18:18)
Old age (16:31; 17:6; 20:29)

Partiality (18:5, 24:23b-25; 28:21)

Pride and humility (3:34b; 8:13; 11:2; 15:33;
16:5, 18, 19; 18:12; 22:4; 29:23)

Reputation (10:7, 22:1)

The righteous man and the wicked man
contrasted (3:32, 33; 10:3, 6, 7, 9, 11, 16,
24, 25, 28, 29-32; 11:3-11, 17-21, 23, 27,
31; 12:2, 3, 5-8, 12-14, 20, 21, 26, 28;
13:2, 5, 6, 9, 21, 25; 14:2, 9, 11, 14, 22, 32;
15:8, 9, 26; 24:15, 16; 28:1, 12)

The scorner or scoffer (3:34a; 9:7, 8, 12; 13:1;
14:6; 15:12; 19:25; 21:11, 24; 22:10; 24:9,
29:8a)

Servants and slaves (14:35; 17:2; 19:10;
29:19, 21)

The sluggard (6:6-11; 10:26; 15:19; 18:9;
19:15, 24; 20:4, 13; 21:25; 22:13; 24:30-
34; 26:13-16)

Soul-winning (11:30; 24:11, 12)

Strife and contention) 10:12, 12:18; 13:10;
15:1-4, 18; 16:27, 28; 18:6-8; 21:9, 19;
28:25)

Suretyship (6:1-5; 11:15; 17:18; 20:16; 22:26,
27; 27:13) Instruction and correction (1:5;
9:7-9; 10:17; 12:1, 15; 13:1, 10, 18, 15:5,
10, 12, 31, 32; 17:10; 19:20, 25; 21:11;
25:12; 27:5, 6, 28:23; 29:1)

Temper and patience (14:17, 29; 15:18;
16:32; 19:11)

Temperance and self-control (23:1-3; 25:28)

Wine (20:1; 21:17; 23:20, 21, 29-35; 31:4-7)

The wisdom of getting guidance or advice from others (11:14; 12:15; 15:22; 20:18; 24:6)

Wisdom personified (1:20-33; 8:1-36; 9:1-6; 14:1a; 16:16, 22; 19:23)

The wise man and foolish man contrasted (3:35; 10:8, 13, 14, 23; 12:15, 16, 23; 13:16; 14:3, 8, 15, 16, 18, 19, 24, 33; 15:7, 14, 20, 21; 17:11, 12, 16, 21, 24, 25, 28; 18:2, 6-8; 29:8, 9, 11)

The Word and obedience to it (13:13, 14; 16:20; 19:16; 28:4, 7, 9; 29:18; 30:5, 6)

Wealth

Accompanied by trouble (15:6, 16, 17; 16:8; 17:1)

Brings friends (19:4, 6)

Gained by violence (11:16)

Gained dishonestly (10:2; 13:22b; 15:6b; 20:17, 21:6, 22:16, 28:8)

Gained hastily (13:11; 20:21; 28:20b, 22)

Gained honestly (10:16)

Gifts and bribes (15:27; 17:8, 23; 18:16; 19:6; 21:14; 25:14; 29:4)

Inherited (19:14)

Its limited value (11:4) Less valuable than wisdom (16:16)

Not to be trusted (11:28)
Pretended (13:7)
Protection of (10:15a; 13:8; 18:11)
Stewardship and generosity (3:9, 10, 27, 28;
    11:24-26; 19:6; 21:26b; 22:9; 28:27)
The rich man and the poor man (10:15: 13:7,
    8; 14:20, 21, 31; 15:16; 17:1, 5: 18:23;
    19:1, 4, 17; 21:13: 22:2, 7, 16, 22, 23; 28:3,
    6, 11, 27: 29:7, 13)

The Wicked Woman
The wicked woman or harlot (2:16-19; 5:3-23;
    6:24-35; 7:5-27; 9:13-18; 22:14; 23:27, 28;
    30:20)

Other Women
A beautiful woman without discretion (11:22)
A contentious woman (19:13; 21:9, 19; 25:24;
    27:15, 16)
A good wife (12:4; 18:22; 31:10-31)
A gracious woman (11:16)
A prudent wife (19:14)
An unloved woman (30:23)
The wife of one's youth (5:18, 19)

26

CHAPTER 4

THE INSTRUCTIONS

1. Materials needed: A Bible, a journal, and a pen.

2. Read the Proverb that corresponds to the numerical day of the month. For example, on the 3rd day of the month you would read Proverbs chapter 3.

3. Write down the verse that jumps off the page for you, or the one that God seems to supernaturally highlight.

4. Write down in your journal a description and/or a devotion on what the verse is saying to you personally.

5. Read the verse that jumped off the page for me and it's corresponding commentary for potentially greater insight to the Proverb.

The format of our Biblical reading routine will be as follows:

Whatever day of the month it is, we will read that corresponding Proverbs chapter. So on the 1st day of the month, we will read Proverbs 1. The 2nd day of the month, we will read Proverbs 2, and so on, and so on.

As you read the chapter, the Holy Spirit will highlight something for you personally. I have captured the verse that jumped off the page for me along with a short devotional. You will first write your devotion in a journal prior to reading my devotion.

You can refer to this journal to see how God is moving in your life and whether or not you are growing closer to Him. I can promise you this, reading the Proverbs every day will absolutely change your life for the better. You will be influenced by THE greatest book on the subject of wisdom ever written.

CHAPTER 5

RABBI'S DAILY JOURNAL OF PROVERBS

As we begin our journey, allow me to pray: *Heavenly Father, I come before You in the name of Yeshua. I humbly ask that You would use this book to draw us closer to You. May the Proverbs mold us, shape us, and change us to become more like Yeshua. It's in Yeshua's name I pray. Amen.*

Let's go!

30

Day 1 – The Purpose of Proverbs

Proverbs 1:10

My son, if sinners entice you, don't go along with them.

It's hard to believe we are living in a day and age of such anarchy and senseless acts of violence. When I was a little boy, people didn't harm people just for sport. It's crazy to think that people are committing random acts of violence on innocent bystanders for no reason whatsoever. They even seem to be enjoying it. We are told that in the last days, people will consider nothing sacred. They will scoff at God. They will be unloving, unforgiving, and have no self-control. My child, if sinners entice you, turn your back on them. Walk in the ways of the righteous. Run from the wicked. Let wisdom be your guide. Often when a young man ruins his life, the explanation is given that he "got in with the wrong crowd." The process is described in verses 10-19 in living color. First, however, the warning flag is flown. Life is full of enticements to evil. We must have the courage and backbone to say "No" a thousand times over.

Day 2 – Wisdom's Ways

Proverbs 2:11

Discretion will watch over you, and discernment will guard you.

This was a tough one. It seemed as though each and every verse was chock full of wisdom. The title of this Proverb should be – The Benefits of Wisdom. If I had to choose one verse that grabbed me, it would be verse 11. It basically states that wise choices will guard you. The word, guard, in Hebrew is *Shaw-mar*. It basically means to keep you, to protect you, and to save your life. We do in fact have the freedom of choice. Each and every day we make choice after choice. These choices all have ramifications. Some will protect us, and others will destroy us. Some will keep us, and others will fail us. Some will save us, and others will lose us. Choose wisdom and live!

Day 3 – Wisdom's Rewards

Proverbs 3:3

Do not let grace and truth leave you — bind them around your neck; write them on the tablet of your heart.

This entire Proverb is absolutely magnificent and all about trusting in the Lord. We find the Bible within the Bible in Proverbs 3:5-6. We read about *Aitz Chaim*, the "Tree of Life", in Proverbs 3:18. And we learn that the Lord curses the wicked but blesses the righteous in Proverbs 3:33. But what jumped off the page for me was Proverbs 3:3, the command to hold onto kindness and faithfulness or grace and truth. We are commanded to bind them around our necks, and to write them down on our hearts. This figurative language is so rich in its symbolism, meaning to hold onto them for dear life. If we are full of grace and kind to others, and we are faithful and true to God, we will find favor with God and man. Today I choose to walk in grace and truth. Hopefully I will do so tomorrow as well.

Day 4 – A Father's Wise Advice

Proverbs 4:10

Listen, my son, receive what I say, and the years of your life will be many.

When I was young, I always dreamt about being a father. I was a man's man, so naturally I wanted a son. When we had our first child, I was ecstatic. I was going to teach him everything there was to know about how to have a good, prosperous, and long life. I was 35 years old when our first son was born, and I had a tremendous amount of life's experiences under my belt. I had made some wonderful choices in my life, and by the same token, I made my fair share of mistakes. I thought that I could clearly correct these wrongs in my child. I was convinced that all he had to do was follow my instructions and life's problems would be averted. Well, that was the plan anyway. Then the reality of a person's own free will and decision-making came into view. I realized that sadly enough, human nature learns from experience. Experience, however, is not our best teacher, wisdom is. Getting wisdom is the wisest thing one can do.

Don't turn your back on wisdom, for she will protect you. Love wisdom, and she will guard you.

Having finished quoting his father's counsel, Solomon now resumes his appeal to his own son. It is a general rule though, not without exception, that a clean life is conducive to a long life. Just think about how tobacco, alcohol, drugs, and sexual sin are directly linked with disease and death. Choose Wisdom and choose life!

Day 5 – Avoid Immoral Women

Proverbs 5:8

Distance your way from her, stay far from the door of her house.

This entire chapter is warning to stay away from sexual immorality. This sin is spoken about over and over again in the Bible. I have seen my share of devout brothers in the Lord fall to what I call the 3 G's, Gold, Glory, and Girls. Obviously this Proverb focuses on the latter. Look at the great King David. Although he did repent of his sins, and God called him a man after His heart, his escapade with Bathsheba marred his reputation, and caused him great pain and sorrow. The fact is, no one is immune and that includes you and me. What follows in verses 9-10 is a bold and frightening warning. It says merciless people, who we are in no shortage of, will come out of the woodwork and devour all you have achieved. That means you can maintain a stellar record for decades, and because of one major bad choice, you can go out at the very bottom. One must ask oneself in all situations, "Is it worth it?" Don't give up what you want most, for what you want at the moment.

Day 6 – Lessons For Daily Life

Proverbs 6:32

He who commits adultery lacks sense; he who does it destroys himself.

Adultery is one of the most frequently and severely condemned sins in the Bible. Adultery is mentioned 52 times, including in the Ten Commandments, all four Gospels, and ten other books of the Bible. Only the sins of idolatry, self-righteousness, and murder are mentioned more often. I don't think we consider the lasting damage adultery causes. The damage is so severe that no amount of repentance can undo it. It is horrifically damaging to the spouse. It often leads to divorce and leaves married couples embittered, untrusting, disillusioned, and financially poorer.

It robs the children of love and the security provided by a healthy, functioning family and gives them a poor role model for their own future marriages. Children from families where there is divorce are more prone to anxiety, poor grades in school, drug and/or alcohol abuse, and delinquency. These problems tend to follow them into adulthood.

Adult children of divorced parents tend to have lower educational attainment, lower income, more children out of wedlock, higher rates of divorce themselves, and a lower sense of wellbeing, according to Charles L. Bryner, Jr. MD in his paper entitled "Children of Divorce." *

All this to say that the potential damage and negative ramifications is enough to warrant any, and all of us, to take very seriously the covenant of Marriage. Maybe that is why the seventh commandment says very succinctly you must not commit adultery, not just don't, but you must not! It's poison, and Proverbs six lays it out there for us plainly. Today we have minimized it like every other sin. It doesn't help when we renamed it an "affair." We desperately need to come back to a place where God is feared. For the fear of the Lord is the very beginning of wisdom.

* Bryner CL Jr., MD, Children of divorce, *The Journal of the American Board of Family Practice,* 2001 May-Jun; 14(3):201-10. PMID: 11355053.

Day 7 – Another Warning About Immoral Women

Proverbs 7:4

Say to wisdom, "You are my sister"; call understanding your kinswoman.

Family is very special. Growing up we spent every weekend with relatives. Our family unit was very close knit. Our immediate family was always together. It afforded me the security needed to become a solid functional human being. I always felt safe and happy with family. I've tried my best to indoctrinate these very principles with my own family as well. The Proverb tells us to love wisdom like a sister and to make insights a beloved member of your family. Love wisdom, live wisdom, treasure wisdom. It's the thread that runs through the entire Bible. "Obey my commands," wisdom says, "and live." This should be the thread that runs through our entire lives as well.

Day 8 – Wisdom Personified

Proverb 8:1-2

Wisdom is calling! Understanding is raising her voice! On the heights along the road, where the paths meet, she is standing.

You get this picture of a man walking along the path and all of a sudden he comes to a crossroads. He has to choose to go one-way or the other. A crossroad is the place where roads intersect. Figuratively it is a point at which a vital decision must be made. Psychology today tells us that the average person makes approximately 35,000 decisions daily. In fact, researchers at Cornell University tell us that the average person makes 266 decisions daily about food alone. Now it is one thing to waver whether you're going to eat pizza or tacos for lunch. It's quite another thing to think about marrying a particular person or not. There are many times when we are at a crossroad in our life where God is directing us in one particular direction, and the tempter is trying to steer us in a different direction. This is when wisdom raises her voice and yells "Go this way!" The Holy Spirit becomes the voice of wisdom. How thankful and appreciative we should be to have the voice of God in our lives to help guide us along the right paths in life. Sadly enough, no matter how loud the voice may be, it cannot force us in a direction we refuse to go. With this being said, we must not trust our instincts, our heart, or our gut. We must trust the Lord! And in so doing, we will find abundant life. For wisdom is the way.

Day 9 – Invitations From Wisdom and Folly

Proverbs 9:7-8

"He who corrects a scoffer only gets insulted; reproving a wicked man becomes his blemish. If you reprove a scoffer, he will hate you; if you reprove a wise man, he will love you.

I think we may spend too much time trying to rebuke the world. In fact, politics has become the new religion. The world has its own kingdom. It has its own culture, its own literature, and its own music, art, lifestyles, and thought patterns. We are in this world, but not of this world. Our citizenship is in Heaven, and likewise our focus is on things above, not on things below. We are called to walk in wisdom. It's the truly wise who welcome reproof. For it takes wisdom for the wise to become all the wiser. To be able to discern between good and evil, and then to walk out the good, is about as wise as it gets. The way in which a man receives rebuke is an index of his character. A scoffer hates you, whereas a wise man will thank you. How do you react when a parent, teacher, employer, or friend corrects you? Instead of resenting criticism, a wise man takes it to heart and thus becomes wiser still.

Day 10 – Righteous and Wicked Lifestyles

Proverbs 10:7

The memory of the righteous will be for a blessing, but the reputation of the wicked will rot.

When we think of a person's name, we tend to think in basic terms. However, in the Bible a good name is better chosen than silver or gold. This does not necessarily refer to a formal name only, but to a person's reputation as well. For instance, it is a rarity to name a child Judas or Jezebel, due to the name's association. Yet, names like Jacob and Rachel are used frequently. One last thing regarding happy memories of the godly. Ask yourself, of the 12 Hebrew spies sent into Canaan, how many can you name? Exactly, Joshua and Caleb. I rest my case.

Day 11 – Pride and Humility

Proverbs 11:2

First comes pride, then disgrace; but with the humble is wisdom.

The Lord makes another great contrast here. Pride and humility are placed on opposite ends of the spiritual spectrum. In fact, pride and humility are polar opposites. I believe we are all more than aware of this, however, pride is insidious, and little by little it spreads like a spiritual cancer. Pride is the father of all sins; therefore, there is absolutely nothing spiritually beneficial about it. It is falling under the false assumption that we know better than God. That is why these Proverbs are so precious and indispensable for one's spiritual growth. Yeshua Himself not only declared His humility, but He showed His humility. He only did what the Father told Him to do, even when it came to dying a criminal's death, by placing Himself as a substitutionary sacrifice on the behalf of ungodly, unappreciative sinners. It's hard to wrap our minds around the magnitude of it all.

In all cases, pride will lead a person to disgrace. Whether it is falsely thinking one knows it all, or thinking that we are entitled and deserving, or just the foolish pride in leaning on one's own understanding. In any and every case pride leads to destruction. Humility on the other hand, not only leads to blessing and honor, but wisdom as well. When we submit our decisions, our desires, and our very lives to the Lord, we are assured to walk in wisdom. All that has been said is absolutely and unequivocally correct. The hard part is putting what we know to be right into practice. I think it all comes down to what we love, and what we want most. God help us!

Day 12 – Hard Work and Laziness

Proverbs 12:11

He who farms his land will have plenty of food, but he who follows futilities has no sense.

Once again, the book of Proverbs never ceases to amaze me. As I read the 28 verses within Proverbs 12, I am astounded by its simple, yet profound wisdom. If I had to use one word to define the book of Proverbs, it would be the word *sublime*. I have never read anything like it, so incredibly practical. This one particular verse did jump off the page for me. We live in a day and age where hard, conscientious laborers are as scarce as hen's teeth. Today it's all about being happy, as opposed to being worthy. Young people today fantasize about their "dream" job. Well, I say wake up from your slumber young person. And that goes double for those who are spiritually lazy. Over and over again Proverbs speaks of the demise of the lazy.

My Dad was ten years old when the Great Depression hit. He was 18 when he became a ranger in WWII. He was awarded the Bronze Star for Bravery, The Purple Heart, and a Marksmen Medal. You can only imagine how hard of a worker he was. He had a very mundane, laborious job that was mindless. Sick or not, he got up every morning at 4 AM and went to work. I never ever heard the man complain, nor talk about his "dream" job. And he didn't believe in luck. In fact, he said to me that his theory on luck was the harder you work, the luckier you get, so there you have it. Unbeknownst to him, he adhered to Proverbs 12:11, some 3,000 years later. A man who engages in positive, constructive work will have his needs supplied. But the man who spends his time in worthless pursuits not only has an empty cupboard but an empty head as well.

Day 13 – Disciplining Your Child

Proverbs 13:24

He who fails to use a stick hates his son, but he who loves him is careful to discipline him.

When it comes to child rearing, things have changed drastically over time. 3,000 years ago God tells us that those who spare the rod hate their children. Those who love their children care enough to discipline them. I sometimes see the extremes when it comes to this tutelage. You either see the pacifistic parent who believes physical disciplining is harsh and abusive, or the exasperated parent who disciplines in anger and for every little falter. The Bible predicts that in the end days people will be disobedient to their parents. Some of the older generations can't understand how parents today let their children speak to them the way they do. One of the problems I see is one of maturity. When I was young, there was somewhat of a generation gap. Parents were figures of authority, and children were expected to submit to that authority. Because parents today don't want to grow up and assume the role of the authoritarian, they end up being their child's friend. This is a huge mistake. Proverbs tells us that familiarity breeds contempt.

I believe Proverbs is telling us that being a loving, caring, compassionate parent is in fact a parent that disciplines his or her children. If a tree starts to bend when it is young, and you don't bend it back early on, once it matures it remains bent. Proverbs advice is to direct your children onto the right path, and when they are older, they will not leave it. The Bible teaches corporal punishment, whether the modern "experts" agree or not. To withhold punishment from a child when it is deserved is to encourage the child in sin and thus to contribute to their eventual ruin. The parent who spares his rod might think he is manifesting love, but God says it is hatred. For years Dr. Benjamin Spock encouraged parents to be permissive. After living to see a generation of bratty, pesky children, he admitted that he had been wrong. He said, "Inability to be firm, to my mind, is the commonest problems of parents in America today." He places the blame on the experts — "The child psychiatrists, psychologists, teachers, social workers, and pediatricians like myself."*

* Benjamin Spock, The Tampa Tribune, January 22, 1974.

Day 14 — Life is Messy

Proverbs 14:4

Where there are no oxen, the stalls are clean; but much is produced by the strength of an ox.

I have been on this journey of walking with the Lord and trying to get to know Him for over 30 years now. I don't think a day has gone by that I did not think of Him. I have read my fair share of spiritual books, spiritual articles, and spiritual doctrine. I have heard my fair share of sermons, and I have watched a fair amount of faith-based movies. With all that being said, all I can say is true spiritual growth is messy.

Faith isn't 5 principles or 7 pillars or even 10 tenets. It's not about formulas or cute little sayings. It's messy. If you want to get closer to God, and you want to have a fruitful life, it will take blood, sweat, and tears. It will not be clean and sterile.

I was in the delivery room with my wife as she gave birth to our four children. It was messy to say the least, especially since the first three were delivered naturally. We were into the first delivery with a very detailed birthing plan. We had certain lighting, specific music, and prayers that were to be read.

Well, the plan was tossed out the window as the events progressed. There were nurses running to and fro, the doctor was giving orders, my wife was screaming, not to mention all the "mess" in the room. However, once our child was delivered, they began the cleanup process rather quickly, and the next thing I saw was my wife and baby snuggled up together in bed, and it was glorious.

What I am saying is this: if you want a bountiful harvest in serving the Lord, prepare to get dirty. A barn can be kept clean and swept where there are no oxen, but isn't it better to have some dust and dirt around, knowing that the labor of an ox will lead to a bountiful harvest? The rewards of toil far outweigh its disagreeable aspects.

Day 15 – Love is Better Than Riches

Proverbs 15:17

Better a vegetable dinner with love than a stall-fattened ox with hate.

This one leaped off the page today. It was in fact my mother's favorite Proverb. She would tell it to me over and over again as a little boy, however, she would put a modern spin on it. Growing up in the Bronx there was a fast-food hamburger chain known as White Castle. I believe it is similar to Krystal's in other parts of the country… at any rate, the hamburger was quite tasty, and it cost just about 15 cents.

There was also a high-end well-known restaurant in Manhattan, called Sign of The Dove, which opened its door in 1962. My mom would say, "My son, better to eat at White Castle with someone you love, than to eat at Sign of The Dove with someone you don't." Well, all this to say, life is not always about the destination or the journey, but rather who you are traveling with.

With all the best friends I have had, there is one that has stuck closer than a brother. His name is Yeshua. I have had the greatest 30 years being with

Him. He has been there on the mountain top with me as well as death's dark ravines. This is why our walk is not external, religious rituals but internal, relational reality.

Make Yeshua your Lord and Savior, and He will be your best friend as well. For Yeshua left, but He's still here. He's returning yet He remains. Never forget His precious words, "I will be with you, always, yes even until the end of the age." (Matt. 28:20)

Day 16 – God is in Control

Proverbs 16:33

One can cast lots into one's lap, but the decision comes from ADONAI.

As I was reading through Proverbs 16, so many wonderful things jumped out at me. I was familiar with many of them. I read and read and then the last sentence spoke to me. This is such a powerful and yet comforting statement if you truly believe it. It is basically saying that God is not only in control of all things, but He is in fact controlling ALL things. Every decision is from the Lord. God either permits or promotes all things.

I think of the story of Purim when I read this Proverb. It was the 5th Century B.C., and the Jewish people were caught between a rock and hard place when they were threatened to be annihilated by the Persian Empire under King Xerxes. He cast the pur, or the lot, basically ancient dice to determine on what day the Jewish people would be exterminated. Although he threw the dice, the Lord determined how they fell.

Although at times God might appear to be absent or silent; in actuality, nothing could be further from the Truth. God is, was, and always will be working, whether it's obvious or not. That's why there is no such thing as coincidences, but rather divine incidences. I am thankful that King Xerxes had trouble sleeping that dreaded night some 2500 years ago. But I am all the more thankful that King Yeshua never slumbers, or sleeps. God is awake, alive, and always working for our good. That's why we need to follow His lead. That's why in verse 9 it states that we can make our plans, but the Lord determines our steps. Keep it simple and follow the Leader!

Day 17 – Peace is Better than Riches

Proverb 17:1

Better a dry piece of bread with calm than a house full of food but also full of strife.

I, like so many, can so relate to this Proverb. Peace, quietness, and tranquility is priceless and so hard to come by these days in a world that is so volatile, unstable, and fragile. I can tell you that when I read God's Word in a quiet setting, there is peace personified. I, myself have never been tremendously wealthy, but somehow, I found myself at times around it. Without being braggadocious, I have been on Yachts, flown in private jets, visited exotic islands, and eaten my fair share of gourmet foods. However, without Peace, it is toxic. I believe each and every human being desires peace and quiet whether they know it or not. I just believe many are looking for it in all the wrong places. Interestingly enough, peace is mentioned 333 times in the Bible.

But there is a Peace that surpasses all understanding. It is an inner calm that will dominate your heart. How can one be so serene in the midst of turmoil? The peace that comes from being in a right relationship with God is not the peace of this world. The world's peace depends on favorable circumstances. Yeshua made a distinction when He said, "Peace I leave with you, *My* peace I give you. I don't give to you as the world gives." (John 14:27) It's incredible to witness. I have seen cancer patients go into remission and say, "I am so thankful to God." I have also seen cancer patients dying and in pain and say, "It will be alright. God is good, and I have peace." This is the Peace that "surpasses all understanding" (Phil. 4:7 ESV). Peace with God, and the Peace of God. There's nothing like it.

Day 18 – Truth and Lies

Proverb 18:17

The first to state his case seems right, till the other one comes and cross-examines.

Once again, I am amazed at just how wise these Proverbs are. 24 verses within the body of Proverbs 18, and every one of them irrefutably wise. With that being said, the 17th verse screams with Truth. I've seen this played out over and over again in life and in ministry. It has been a Proverb I have lived by.

Although I find that truth is absolute, perspective is not. Now, there are some who are out and out liars. They manipulate others through misrepresentation of the facts. Then there are others who just aren't able to see things objectively. They have their perspective and, although they believe it to be true, there may be another perspective to be listened to. This in essence is the word of wisdom here. The first to speak up in court sounds right, until the cross examination begins.

So, if I hear something, I have no good reason not to believe it, and yet I have no good reason to believe it. I must have the information corroborated. This is why the Bible in Deuteronomy says a man cannot be convicted of a crime based on the testimony of just one witness. In my travels, I have discovered that there are usually three sides to every story: two distinct perspectives and then there is the truth.

This is why I just love the Bible. Everything is magnificently contrasted in just two categories. The truth and the lie. At the end of the age there will only be two categories as well. There will be the lost and the saved.

Choose Yeshua and choose Life!

Day 19 – People Blame God

Proverbs 19:3

A person's own folly is what ruins his way, but he rages in his heart against ADONAI.

I've always said, I would not want to be God. Why? Because when things go wrong, God gets the blame, and when things go right, man takes the credit. What this verse is basically saying is that people ruin their lives by their own foolish choices, and then they get angry at God for the outcome. And what are these "foolish" choices? Making decisions apart from God's council, or worse yet, outright going against God's commandments.

In verse 16 of the same chapter, God basically states the following: Keep the commandments and keep your life; despising them leads to death. God has instructed us in His love that the commandments are Holy, just, and good. If followed, they lead to prosperity, protection, and peace. They are in all thing's life giving. It's not about surviving but about thriving. It's not about breaking down but breaking through. We don't have to hang in there, because Yeshua already hung up there, and if we appropriate this in and through us, we will not just have everlasting life but abundant life in the here and now. Father knows best!

As a loving parent, we are confident we know what's best for our children. How much more does our Heavenly Father know what's best for us? I Say, if you are making foolish decisions and life is a mess, be man enough to take responsibility for it. The blame game has been played from the very beginning when God said. "Have you eaten from the tree whose fruit I commanded you not to eat?" Then man replied, "It was the woman YOU gave me who gave me the fruit, and I ate it."

Here's some great news: God will still be waiting when the disaster of our choice has taught us the foolishness of that choice.

If and when we own up to our foolishness and decide that we want to go in a different direction, then and only then will God forgive our wrongs and bless us on the road to righteousness.

Do It Today!

Day 20 – God Knows Best

Proverb 20:24

A man's steps are ordered by ADONAI, so how can a person understand his own ways?

You can never ever go wrong following God's lead. He is too loving to be unkind, and too wise to make a mistake. Just as our earthly father wants the best for us, our Heavenly Father wants the best for us all the more. The big difference is God is omniscient and our parents are not. I guess the saying "Father knows best" takes on a whole new meaning for those of us who are born again. This verse emphasizes God's sovereignty and not man's free will, though both are true. The thought is that God is sovereign over human affairs, and He knows what is best for us.

Bottom line, trust the Lord, and stop trying to figure it out.

Day 21 – The Wrong Fight

Proverb 21:30

No wisdom, discernment or counsel succeeds against ADONAI.

Fighting against God is a losing battle. You cannot thwart God's plans. He does what He wants, when He wants, how He wants, where He wants, to whomever He wants. Even the highest and greatest Angel tried to fight God. How did that go? God is omnipotent; God is omniscient; God is omnipresent. God is God, period. It would behoove one and all to choose God's side.

Adam and Eve had access to every single solitary tree in the Garden, except for one. As soon as they ate from the forbidden fruit, they began to die! Ever since then, one out of one still dies. I repeat, fighting against God is a losing battle.

Day 22 – Prevention is Best

Proverbs 22:3

The clever see trouble coming and hide; the simple go on and pay the penalty.

"An ounce of prevention is worth a pound of cure" was said in 1736 by Benjamin Franklin regarding the fact that preventing fires is better than fighting them. It's easier to stop something from happening in the first place than to repair the damage after the fact. Whether you are dealing with an automobile or a human being, preventative maintenance is far superior to extensive repair. As the old saying goes, "You can pay me now, or you can pay me later."

More importantly look at our efforts in raising our children. Setting up boundaries are like the banks of a river. They give the child support and yet allow him or her to flow with strength. If and when the banks weaken, the forceful waters become a putrid pond. Remember an ounce of prevention is worth a pound of cure.

Day 23 – Can't Take It With You

Proverbs 23:4-5

Don't exhaust yourself in pursuit of wealth; be smart enough to desist

If you make your eyes rush at it, it's no longer there! For wealth will surely grow wings, like an eagle flying off to the sky.

My dad used to say, "Kid, there is no luggage rack on a hearse," meaning you can't take it with you. Not only can't you take it with you, but in an instant, it can be taken away from you. Because my dad was ten years of age when the great depression hit, he told me not to look so much to increase my revenue, but to decrease my expenses. Basically, to live under my means. Don't buy things you don't need with money you don't have. What legacy are you going to leave behind, besides wealth and riches? Ask yourself, how much better was the world's Spiritual condition because you were here? Fear God and obey His commandments, for this is the duty of all men!

Day 24 – No Gloating

Proverbs 24:17-18

Don't rejoice when your enemy falls; don't let your heart be glad when he stumbles.

For ADONAI might see it, and it would displease him; he might withdraw his anger from your foe.

The Lord is obviously so merciful. He even asks of us not to gloat and celebrate our enemies stumbling. I think of the Passover Seder when we announce the Plagues by dipping our finger in the glass of wine and placing a droplet of the wine on our plates. As a little child I did not inquire as to the reason behind it.

As I grew up, I came to understand that a full glass of wine represents the fullness of joy. The plagues caused much sorrow. How can we be fully joyful in the midst of such sorrow? We should always remember that our deliverance came to us at a huge price. May we never forget the price Yeshua paid for our sins. Remember, freedom isn't free!

Day 25 – Weep With Those Who Weep

Proverbs 25:20

Like removing clothes on a chilly day or like vinegar on soda is someone who sings songs to a heavy heart.

When a person is going through it, struggling in life, and is downright sad, they are not looking for someone to come and just cheer them up. They are looking for someone to understand their situation and for that someone to have empathy. Sometimes crying with another is far better than trying to give them a remedy.

When a person dies in Orthodox Judaism, the survivors sit shiva for seven days. They mourn in an fairly austere fashion. I remember sitting Shiva when my dad died. For those paying a shiva call, we are told not to say much at all. If the person who lost their loved one wants to talk, let them lead the conversation. This way you can meet them where they are and not where you think they should be. Mourning is very personal.

There is a story about a minister making his first hospital visit. He found the poor patient with both legs strung up to pulleys, both arms in plaster, and an IV in one of them. He said with his big evangelical smile, "Brother, are you rejoicing?" I have a feeling that whatever the patient said, it wasn't very polite.

Day 26 – No Haphazard Curses

Proverbs 26:2

Like a fluttering sparrow or a flying swallow, an undeserved curse will come home to roost.

The Bible speaks of blessings and curses. It doesn't appear that there is any neutrality. It seems that all we think, say, and do has a positive or negative result. God classifies blessings as tied into obedience, and curses as tied into disobedience. Doing what's "right" will result in goodness and doing what's "wrong" will result in badness. All things considered, this is pretty cut and dried

The good news is that here in the book of Proverbs, we are told that there are no haphazard curses. God does not permit or promote random curses. You can rest assured that the good things we do will bring forth blessing on ourselves and on others. Sadly enough, the opposite is true as well. The bad things we do will bring forth curses on ourselves and on others. You can never go wrong doing the right thing!

Proverbs 26:2

Like a fluttering sparrow or a flying swallow,
an undeserved curse will come home to roost.

Day 27 – Inside, We're All Similar

Proverbs 27:19

Just as water reflects the face, so one human heart reflects another.

As you look into a clear pool, you see your face reflected in the water. Even so, as you study other people, you see much that you find in yourself. The same emotions, temptations, ambitions, thoughts, strengths, and weaknesses.

That is why it happens that if a man preaches to himself, he is surprised by how many other people he hits.

Day 28 – Keep Torah!

Proverbs 28:4

Those who abandon Torah praise the wicked, but those who keep Torah fight them.

No one in their right mind would want to praise wickedness, especially those who belong to the family of faith. In actuality, if we loved the Lord, we would hate evil. In fact, we are told, "The fear of the Lord is to hate evil" (Prov. 8:13 NASB). How do we fight the wicked? Simply by obeying the law. Every time we say yes to God, we are praising Him.

I really believe the best way to sing our Hallelujahs is to live an obedient life. The greatest sermon ever spoken is an obedient life. Obey, obey, obey. It's the only way!

Day 29 – Godly Leaders, Better for All

Proverbs 29: 2

When the righteous flourish, the people rejoice; but when the wicked are in power, the people groan.

This holds true throughout history. Empires under men like Stalin, Mussolini, and Hitler were horrific. Why? When evil men are in authority, sin flourishes. Sin was the problem; sin is the problem, and sin will always be the problem. Sin steals, sin murders, sin destroys. The devil who is evil personified comes to rob, kill, and destroy.

The Lord comes to bring life, and life more abundantly. When God fearers are in authority, the people rejoice. You and I are all in positions of authority. We should always maintain our position with righteousness. It's a win, win, win. God gets Glorified, the people prosper, and we receive honor and blessing. Hallelujah!

Day 30 – What is His Son's Name?

Proverbs 30:4 – The sayings of Agur

Who has gone up to heaven and come down? Who has cupped the wind in the palms of his hands? Who has wrapped up the waters in his cloak? Who established all the ends of the earth? What is his name, and what is his son's name? Surely you know!

We are asked questions. We then get these questions answered. In the Torah, Exodus 15:10; In the writings, Job 26:8; In the Psalms, Psalm 24:2; and in the Prophets, Isaiah 45:18.

It's the last question that is most important, "What is His Name — and His son's name?" Tell me if you know! Our hands should be raised high, jumping up and down and exclaiming at the top of our lungs, "Ooh, ooh, pick me!"

YUD-HEY-VAV-HEY is His name, Elohim, The Creator and Sustainer of the universe. The great I AM. The causeless cause, our Heavenly Father. And His Son's Name, Yeshua the Messiah.

Revelation chapter 19 verse 12 says, "His eyes were like a fiery flame, and on his head were many royal crowns. And He had a name written which no one

knew but Himself." Until then let us praise the Father
and His Son!

Day 31 – Proverbs 31 Woman

Proverbs 31:26

When she opens her mouth, she speaks wisely; on her tongue is loving instruction.

This was a tough one for myself. When a person thinks of Proverbs 31, they immediately gravitate to the latter part of the Proverbs which speaks of a wife of noble character. It has been so well taught, that women of noble character are referred to as a Proverbs 31 woman. I personally had the distinct joy of being raised by a legitimate Proverbs 31 woman, in every sense of the word. I could go on and on about my mom and her noble character. I think what I wrote on her headstone says it all, "Here lies one in seven billion."

Not only did I have the opportunity of being raised by a Proverbs 31 woman but by the Grace of God, I married a Proverbs 31 woman.

I hope and pray all reading this can relate to it personally. Every verse in this Proverb is checked off by my wife's character. But one verse jumps off the page when I think of my wife and that is verse 26. Not only is she beautiful inside and out, not only is she incredibly hard working and resourceful, but she speaks Pearls of Wisdom, and she gives instructions with kindness. They say men sometimes look to marry someone like their mothers. All I can say is, "Thank you, Mom; thank you, Bern; and thank You, God.

CHAPTER 6

IN CONCLUSION

There is nothing that has ever been penned in all human history that compares to the book of Proverbs. Why? Because it is incomparable in its ability to state simplistically what one needs to do in order to live a protected, prosperous, and peaceful life. When one buys a particular product, it is always wise to check the manufacturer's label, or the manufacturer's manual. For whom better to check with than the manufacturer of the product themselves.

When it comes to our lives, it would be wiser still to check with the manufacturer, and His "manual." The book of Proverbs is a manual for living like none other. But just to issue a word of caution, it's not enough to read the manual. One must implement what's written in the manual. In other words, don't just read it, do it!

I believe with all my heart, human beings really want to be happy. They want to feel a sense of security. They want to prosper, and they definitely want to experience peace. Well, after you have exhausted all avenues, and you have still come up short, may I suggest life's manual, the Book of Proverbs. By applying its principles, not only will you avoid the pitfalls in life, but you shall experience the summits as well.

Other books by the author:

FROM THE PROJECTS TO THE PALACE

*A LIFE FOR GOD a Rabbi's Analysis of
the Cross, Life, and Eternity.*

www.ingramcontent.com/pod-product-compliance
Lightning Source LLC
Chambersburg PA
CBHW070001100426
42741CB00012B/3099